Rolf W. Roth

Lost in the USA

Ernst Klett Verlag
Stuttgart Düsseldorf Leipzig

Zu dieser Lektüre gibt es eine Kassette
(Klettnummer 572321)

1. Auflage A 1 11 10 9 8 | 2006 05 04 03

Alle Drucke dieser Auflage können im Unterricht nebeneinander benutzt werden. Die letzte Zahl bezeichnet das Jahr dieses Druckes.

Internetadresse: http://www.klett-verlag.de

Zeichnungen: Peter Gray, London.
Druck: Wilhelm Röck, Weinsberg.
Printed in Germany.

ISBN 3-12-572320-5

Contents

Chapter 1

It was two days before the Easter holidays, and Frank was sitting in his English lesson. On the desk in front of him there was an open exercise book. The two pages looked completely red, and there was a big 6 at the end of the text.

"I'm sorry, Frank, but you made a lot of mistakes," Frau Peters, his English teacher, said and smiled at him, but Frank did not smile back. There were tears in his eyes when he looked up at her.

"I'm sorry, Frank," Frau Peters said again and walked away quickly. There were tears in her eyes, too. Poor Frank. He had no idea about English and she just didn't know how to help him. There were too many things he didn't know and understand. There was no way he could still learn everything now. It was just too late for him. He would be in the 7th grade again next year.

"Have lots of fun in the holidays," Frau Peters said just before the bell rang. "I want you to tell me about everything when you come back – in English, of course."

Frank got up slowly. That was another problem: nothing exciting ever happened to him in the holidays – everybody knew that – not like to Jessica, who always became billiard champion in a hotel somewhere in Turkey, or Michael, who always went to Spain with his mother ... Well, and even if something ever happened to him, he wouldn't be able to talk about it *in English.*

7 **tear** [tɪə] — Träne
15 **grade** [greɪd] *(AE)* — *hier:* Jahrgang, Klasse
22 **champion** ['tʃæmpɪən] — Sieger, Meister

But there was no danger of that. He wasn't going to go anywhere. Since they had their new house, there was no money for holidays. That's what his parents said. So they weren't going anywhere at Easter.

At home, Frank didn't want to show his parents the test – and when he finally did, they tried not to be angry ...

That night in bed Frank heard his parents. They were still talking about his English marks. It was especially at times like this that he wished he had a brother or sister.

"He's much too young," he heard his mother say then.

"He's 13 now," his father said.

"Yes, but he isn't very sure of himself. I wish we could go with him."

"But we can't, and perhaps it's better if he goes alone. Well, we have to see first if it's possible, and we have to talk to Frank, too."

Frank was puzzled. What were they talking about? He slept a little then, but woke up later again. His mother was on the phone now and she was talking to someone about him. He tried to listen but couldn't understand what she was saying.

In the morning he found out: Frank could spend the Easter holidays with his aunt in America. He would fly there alone and stay with Aunt Trudy. She would try to speak only English with him while he was there, and maybe he would learn a little bit.

9 **to wish** [wɪʃ] wünschen
17 **puzzled** [ˈpʌzld] verdutzt, verwirrt

Aunt Trudy in America? Frank was worried. He didn't really know her. She was his mother's sister but she had been in America for a long time. Frank had only seen her once many years ago. And he had never been away from home before – at least not like this. But he said 'yes'. His English really *was* bad.

Frank left Germany on the first day of the holidays. It was difficult at the airport. His parents tried not to look or act worried, but Frank knew they were and so was he. He had to fly to New York City, and then he had to change planes there. Someone from the airline would help him, and in Oklahoma City Aunt Trudy would be at the airport to meet him.

On the plane, Frank's neighbours spoke to him *in English* and Frank didn't know what to do. Then he found the headphones and put them on ... and later he slept.

But then at Kennedy Airport in New York City it was strange. It was afternoon – almost the same time as when he'd left Germany. And now he was in a different world.

Everyone was speaking English all around him and he felt completely lost. But then a lady from the airline took him outside the building and pointed to a bus. "Just get on that big one there. It will take you to the other airline. Someone will be there waiting for you. They will help you."

"Er – what?" Frank said.

11 **airline** ['eəlaɪn] Fluglinie
22 **building** ['bɪldɪŋ] Gebäude
22 **to point** ['pɔɪnt] **to s.th.** auf etwas zeigen

The lady smiled at him. "The big bus," she said, pointed again and left. She seemed to be in a hurry.

Frank looked around. Which bus did she mean? There was a black bus – a van – with the side door open near him. Was that the right one? Quickly he got into it. Strange, there were no seats or windows. It was dark and there were some big bundles and some very loud music from the driver's cabin. No, this couldn't be right. Frank started to get out again but fell over a bundle. He tried to get up, but someone slammed the door then, and Frank fell down again – in the dark. Quickly he climbed over the bundles and knocked against the wall between him and the driver and shouted, but the music was too loud. The van kept on moving.

Frank was scared and tried to open the door but couldn't find the handle. Anyway, the van was going fast now and he decided to wait until it stopped. Maybe it *was* the right bus; he hoped it was and that he would be on his flight to Oklahoma City soon ...

6	**dark** [dɑ:k]	dunkel
7	**bundle** ['bʌndl]	Bündel
8	**cabin** ['kæbɪn]	*hier:* Führerhaus
10	**to slam** [slæm]	zuschlagen
11	**to knock** [nɒk]	klopfen
15	**handle** ['hændl]	(Tür)griff

Chapter 2

In a garage on West 60th Street in Manhattan, two men were waiting.

The tall thin one talked to someone on a mobile phone, then put it away.

"Good news," he said. "Everything went all right. Pancho will be here soon now."

"Great!" the other man shouted. "With those exotic furs we'll be in the money."

"Yeah, and don't forget these diamonds here," Smitty, the thin man, said and touched a pouch he had around his neck. "We'll be OK for the rest of our lives now."

A few minutes later the big garage door opened and the black van drove in. The driver turned off his music and closed the garage door with the remote control.

"Good work, Pancho," Smitty said.

"No problem," Pancho smiled with big teeth, and that's when they heard the noise inside the van.

"Hey, what's that?" Fats said. He was a fat black man.

When they got the door open, the three men and Frank looked at each other.

"Who's this?" the thin man said to Pancho.

3	**tall** [tɔ:l]	groß
3	**thin** [θɪn]	dünn
7	**fur** [fɜ:]	Pelz
10	**to touch** [tʌtʃ]	berühren, anfassen
10	**pouch** [paʊtʃ]	(Brust)beutel
11	**neck**	Hals
14	**remote control** [rɪ'məʊt kən'trəʊl]	Fernbedienung
18	**fat** [fæt]	dick

"No idea! Hey, who are you, kid?" Pancho said. He had a Spanish accent.

Frank looked around. Was he still at the airport? "Er – who am I?" he asked.

"That's what we want to know. Who are you?" Fats smiled at him.

"Who – er – yes, *where* am I?" Frank said.

"Hey, this kid is a comic," Smitty said and grabbed Frank. "Here, he's got a passport in his pocket," he said and took it away from Frank.

"No!" Frank shouted. "My – er – my passport!" He tried to take it back, but Pancho held him and laughed.

8 **to grab** [græb] packen, schnappen
9 **passport** ['pɑ:spɔ:t] Reisepass

"Hey, there's some money here, too," Fats picked it up from the floor. "$50 – wow!" he laughed, and put it in his pocket.

"No, my money!" Frank shouted.

"Shut up!" Pancho shook him hard, and Frank was scared.

The thin man looked at Frank's passport and at the ticket in it. "He's a German kid," he said. "How'd he get in the van, Pancho?"

"Don't know. Maybe he came in on a plane and then got in the van by mistake."

"Well, let's get rid of him," the thin man said and put Frank's passport and ticket in the pouch he had around his neck.

"What do you mean, Smitty?" Fats asked.

That's when Frank pulled himself free from Pancho and ran to a door at the side of the garage.

"Quick, get him!" Smitty shouted.

Pancho ran to the door, too, but Fats only laughed, "Ahh, let the kid go. He doesn't know anything. It'll just mean trouble if we try to keep him here."

"We can't take a chance," Smitty said. "He might bring the police here before we can get away with all the stuff."

Outside on the sidewalk now, the three men saw Frank at the end of the street. He was running.

"We have to get him," Smitty said. "We have to."

5	**shut up!**	halt den Schnabel!
5	**to shake**	schütteln
12	**to get rid of**	loswerden
23	**stuff** [stʌf]	Zeug
24	**sidewalk** ['--] *(AE)*	Gehsteig, Gehweg

Frank saw the three men behind him as he ran around the corner. There were skyscrapers everywhere and a big noisy street with a lot of traffic in front of him. No, this was not the airport. The men were coming fast. Frank ran out into the street and a car almost hit him. Then someone shouted at him – but he ran on. Another car had to stop for him, but he got across and ran into a park. But two of the men had crossed the street, too, and were coming after him.

Frank ran as fast as he could. In front of him he saw some bushes. Quickly he went into them and looked out between the leaves. The little fat man and the one with the big teeth had stopped running and were looking around

"Hey," someone suddenly said behind him and Frank nearly jumped out of his skin. An old man was sitting on the ground. "Here, take this," he said and gave Frank a dirty old jacket. "Put this on and walk out of here. Walk! Don't run! They won't know it's you."

Frank looked at him and the old man put a baseball hat on his head. "Those are bad men. I can see that. Just walk, don't run," he said again and smiled at him, and this time Frank understood.

He thanked the man and stepped out of the bushes. He wanted to run but didn't. Pancho and Fats saw him, but the old man had been right. They only stood there and looked in all directions, but they did not follow him. At the corner Frank saw a big building and suddenly he knew what it was: the Plaza Hotel. He'd seen it in that film where the boy was alone in New York. He was in Manhattan!

2 **skyscraper** ['skaɪˌskreɪpə] Wolkenkratzer
10 **bush, bushes** ['bʊʃɪz] Busch, Gebüsch
11 **leaf, leaves** [li:f / li:vz] Blatt, Blätter
25 **direction** [dɪ'rekʃn] Richtung

Frank looked over his shoulder again and saw the two men: they were looking in his direction now but they were not following him. Then he noticed that the little man had a phone and was talking to someone. He ran again then, across the street and into the hotel. Someone tried to stop him, but he ran on. There were a lot of people inside and Frank ran through some large rooms and then out of another door again. Outside he saw a policeman at the next corner and ran towards him, but then suddenly Smitty was there and caught him.

Frank fought, but Pancho and Fats were there, too, now and together they took Frank off the street and back into the park. He tried to shout, but they put a hand over his mouth and no one paid any attention to them.

Back in the building with the garage, they threw away his dirty jacket, took him up to the 35th floor and locked him in an empty room.

Frank was really scared now. There was no way he could get out and when he shouted or kicked against the door no one came to help him. The afternoon sun shone in through the one dirty window but it was locked, too, and 35 floors up.

Outside Frank saw skyscrapers everywhere. Some of them he knew from pictures. The two towers at the end of the island were the World Trade Center. He also recognized the tops of the Empire State Building and the Chrysler Building. Below tiny cars and people moved through the streets ... He touched the baseball hat he still had on his head and felt a little better.

14	**to pay attention** [ə'tenʃn] **to s.th./s.o.**	auf etwas/jdn achten
20	**to shine, shone, shone** [ʃaɪn / ʃɒn]	scheinen
27	**tiny** ['taɪnɪ]	winzig

After a while he lay down on the floor and slept. When he woke up, it was dark and there was food and something to drink next to him. Later Fats came into the room and Frank tried to run out while the door was open, but the little man pushed him back and locked it. Then he talked to Frank, but Frank didn't understand him.

After that it was always Fats who brought him food and he always stayed and talked to Frank. Slowly he began to follow what the man was saying.

Three days later, when Fats told him, "I know this isn't nice for you, kid," Frank answered, "Then just let me go." He said it in English and without thinking about it. It was just natural.

"I wish we could, but we can't," Fats said and left.

Frank felt that Fats wasn't really a bad man – he had even given him his $50 again – but he had to do what Smitty said.

13 **natural** ['nætʃrəl] natürlich

Chapter 3

When Frank did not get off the plane in Oklahoma City, Aunt Trudy was worried and asked the airline a lot of questions. When she got no answers, she called Germany, and there was panic. She called the police next ... Two days later, when they still did not know where Frank was, his parents decided to fly to the US, too.

In the Manhattan apartment, Pancho, Fats and Smitty were packing. The bundles of furs were all in the van now.

"We're ready," Smitty said. "Our plane is waiting for us. We just have to drive to the airport and fly ..." he stopped because Pancho was bringing Frank to the car.

"Can't we let the kid go now?" Fats asked. "We'll be gone, and he can't do anything."

"I don't want to take the chance. We'll take him along on the plane and drop him off somewhere on the way."

"Drop him off?" Fats looked worried and so did Frank although he wasn't sure he had really understood.

The drive to the plane was a long one especially because Pancho always had to stay under the speed limit of 55 m.p.h.

"Slow down, you idiot!" Smitty told him again and again. "We don't want the police to stop us for speeding."

7 **apartment** [ə'pɑ:tmənt] *(AE)* Wohnung
14 **to take s.o. along** jdn mitnehmen
15 **to drop s.o. off** jdn absetzen

In a town named Garrett in the south-west of Pennsylvania they drove to a small private airport and put the furs onto a plane. Then, with Frank tied up in the back, they flew west into the afternoon sun.

Later, when Frank was able to look out of the window all he could see was trees. Hills and trees as far as he could see. In the seat in front of him Fats was sleeping, and on the other side Pancho was looking at Smitty's pouch, the one with his passport in it.

And much later, Smitty, who was flying the plane, said, "This is the place where we can get rid of the kid. Get him ready."

"OK, Frank," Fats said, "this is where you get out."

"Get out?" Frank understood that and became really scared and started to fight and kick, but the two men held him – and then Smitty brought the plane down over the trees.

"That's the clearing over there," he said, flew in and landed the plane.

When it came to a stop on the ground, Pancho opened the door. Then he untied Frank and pulled him over to it. "You're out in the wilderness here," he said, "but if you follow that road over there between the trees," he pointed to it, "you'll get back to civilization sooner or later."

Frank only looked at him.

2 **private** ['praɪvɪt]
3 **to tie up** ['taɪ ˌʌp] — *hier:* fesseln
18 **clearing** — Lichtung
22 **wilderness** ['wɪldənɪs] — Wildnis
24 **civilization** [ˌsɪvɪlaɪ'zeɪʃn]
24 **sooner or later** — früher oder später

Then Fats came over and explained it to him until it was clear.

"OK, push him out," Smitty shouted from the front, and Pancho did.

"By the time he finds someone, we'll be enjoying the good life," Pancho laughed and did not see Frank grab the pouch with his passport in it from the seat just as he fell out.

"Good luck!" Fats came to the door and called down.

Frank lay on the ground as the plane started to move again and took off. In his hand he still held the pouch he had grabbed from the seat. He opened it now and found his passport inside and smiled. He closed it again and put it around his neck, got up and slowly started walking to the road Pancho and Fats had showed him.

"Back to civilization," he said to himself in English. It was early afternoon and very sunny. Where would the road take him? Would he find someone to help him? And what about Aunt Trudy – and his parents? He was sure they already knew that something had happened to him.

It wasn't until much later and after the plane had landed again that the men noticed the pouch was missing. The three of them looked everywhere in the plane again and again before they began to suspect the worst.

"It was on my seat just before we pushed the kid out," Pancho said.

9	**good luck!**	viel Glück!
11	**to take off**	*hier:* abheben
24	**to suspect** [sə'spekt]	*hier:* vermuten

They looked at each other.

"His passport was in it and he wanted it back. His parents probably told him not to lose it. I'm sure he grabbed it," Fats said.

"Never mind his passport! We've got over $500,000 in diamonds in that damn pouch!" Smitty shouted.

"You've got to fly back, boss," Pancho said.

"We can't. We have to get some fuel first."

"Damn!"

6 **damn** [dæm] verdammt
8 **fuel** ['fjʊəl] Treibstoff

Chapter 4

Three hours later Frank got to another road. He was hungry and thirsty and very tired but felt better when he saw that it was a normal road, one for cars. At first he did not know which way to go but finally decided to go to the right. He only hoped that there would be a car soon – and that it would stop. Or perhaps he would find a house.

But even after he had walked another hour there was nothing. No traffic, no houses – nothing. He was all alone. He touched the pouch. At least he had his passport. Frank looked at it. His ticket was in it, and there was something in the bottom of the pouch, too. Some paper. He wanted to take it out but then he noticed something far away – a building – and forgot about the paper.

After they had gotten their fuel, Smitty flew back to the clearing where they had left Frank. He circled the area but they could not see Frank anywhere. In the end Smitty landed on the road Frank had found and let out Pancho and Fats.

"You have to find him," he said. "I'll take the plane somewhere else. We'll stay in contact by phone."

It was getting dark when Frank got to the building. It was a filling station and it was all by itself. There were no houses or anything, just the station. Frank saw a man inside the building and went there quickly.

4	**finally** ['faɪnəlɪ]	am Ende, schließlich
14	**they had gotten** *(AE)*	= they had got
15	**to circle** ['sɜːkl]	*hier:* im Kreis überfliegen
21	**filling station**	Tankstelle
21	**all by itself**	ganz für sich

Pancho and Fats were dead tired when they reached a little town. They went to a small café and had some black coffee.

"He went the other way, I'm sure of that," Pancho said and took his shoes off under the table.

"Yeah, you're right. We have to rent a car and find him."

"OK, but it's probably too late for that. I'm sure he's talked to the police already."

"No," Fats said and shook his head. "He hasn't. Look."

In the corner and above them a TV was on.

"Police have still not found the 13-year-old German boy who got lost at Kennedy Airport four days ago. They have been looking everywhere. Frank's parents are now in Oklahoma City with ..."

"See," Fats said. "He's still out there. He went the other way."

"Yeah, we'll get a car and then we'll find him."

When Pancho and Fats arrived at the filling station, Frank was just coming out of the restroom. He saw the headlights of their car, then heard their voices and stopped. Carefully he looked around the corner and saw them. They were going into the building. What should he do?

"Hi," he heard Pancho's voice. "We're looking for a young boy," he said to the man in the station. "Has he been here?"

1 **dead** *(informal)*	*hier*: sehr
6 **to rent a car** *(AE)*	ein Auto mieten
19 **restroom** *(AE)* ['--]	Toilette
19 **headlights** ['--]	Scheinwerfer (am Auto)

"What? You must speak slowly," the man said. "My English is not so good. I'm from Korea – only here in this country a short time."

"Never mind the family history. What about the boy?" Pancho said.

On the other side of the filling station there was a big open truck with cattle in the back. Frank saw the driver get into the cabin. He started the engine. Frank looked around the corner. Pancho and Fats were still inside, but Frank could hear them. They sounded angry.

"What do you mean?" Pancho shouted. "Did he call somebody or didn't he?"

7 **cattle** ['kætl] Vieh

The filling station man smiled. "He wanted to call, but did not know how. Is he your boy?"

"Well, where is he now?" Fats asked and looked outside.

That's when Frank ran around the building and jumped onto the back of the truck just as it was leaving the filling station. Quickly he climbed over the top and looked down at all the cows below him.

Chapter 5

Frank was sitting on the floor now, in the corner, with the cows' legs everywhere. It was completely dark and the truck was moving faster. Frank pulled the baseball hat down over his face and hoped the men would not catch him.

He had tried to talk to the man at the station, but they had not understood each other. And before he could try to use the phone again, Pancho and Fats arrived.

Frank leaned back against the wood. He was really tired and soon he was asleep.

When he woke up later, the truck was still moving. It was still dark – and he was not alone. Someone was sitting next to him, looking at him. Frank almost shouted ...

Pancho and Fats were in their car again.

"Maybe he got a ride with somebody – we've looked everywhere," Fats said.

"Yeah, wasn't there a truck or something?"

"Right, there was. But where did it go?"

"Let's call Smitty. Maybe he can use the plane to find it."

"Not in the dark he can't."

"Well, let's go."

The other person in the back of the truck was a girl. And as Frank soon found out, her name was Linda and she was his age. She had climbed on the truck when it had stopped in a village. Now she sat next to Frank and they talked.

8 **to lean** [i:] sich anlehnen
9 **asleep** [ə'sli:p] eingeschlafen
23 **age** Alter

"Are you running away from home, too?" she asked him.

"What?" Frank looked at her in the darkness. She had long dark hair and was wearing jeans and a sweatshirt like him.

"Running away," she said. "You know going away from your parents, from home."

"Oh," Frank said. "No – not running away. I want to – er – to go home."

"What do you mean? Where are you from?"

Frank leaned back and tried to explain everything to her. It was very difficult, but Linda seemed to know what he wanted to say and helped him with the words.

"Wow!" she said finally. "What a story! Great the way you got your passport back."

Frank got it out and showed it to her. Then he asked her, "But you're running away? From home?"

"Yes," Linda said. "My mother and father are divorced, but Mom has married again and now we're going to move, and I'll have to go to a boarding school, but I don't want to."

"What's that?"

"It's a school where you live – all the time. You can only go home during the vacations."

"You mean during the school holidays?" Frank asked.

"Yes, that's right," Linda said, and Frank understood.

"Boarding school," he said to himself.

18	**divorced** [dɪ'vɔːst]	geschieden
19	**Mom** *(AE)* [mɒm]	Mama, Mutti
19	**to marry** ['mærɪ]	heiraten
23	**vacation** *(AE)* [və'keɪʃn]	

They talked a lot more then, all through the night. Linda always helped Frank with his English and they became friends.

With the first light of morning the animals became nervous, and soon the truck slowed down.

"Hey, he's turning off the road. Where is he going?"

"Maybe the animals are thirsty," Frank said.

"Yes, I'm sure you're right. He's going to water the cattle somewhere."

"The cattle?"

"These animals here."

Fats was driving the rented car now while Pancho was trying to sleep.

"Damn!" Fats shouted, "That truck has to be on this road."

"What?" Pancho said, waking up.

"I'm sure they've turned off somewhere," Fats told him.

"There isn't any place to go here. This is all empty prairie. Let's call Smitty. He'll have to help us with the plane."

"Damn! He'll be really angry."

The truck was on a small road now. Frank and Linda were standing in the back, at the side, away from the nervous animals. It was light now and Frank could see that the countyside was different here.

"No trees," he said to Linda. "No, er, little mountains."

"No, there are no trees or hills here," she said. "This is big sky country."

5 **to slow down** langsamer fahren

"What's that?"

"Just look," Linda said, and Frank looked out at the land. It was flat and you could see for miles and miles – and above him the sky was big and empty and he felt very small.

"Yes," he said. "Big sky country."

The truck slowed down again, then turned off onto a dirt road and the air became dusty. The two friends sat down and Frank held his hat over his nose.

Much later Linda said, "I think he's going to stop now. We'll have to get down fast and hide or the driver will see us. Then we'll get on again when he's finished."

"OK – get down fast," Frank said, and when the truck was slow enough, they jumped off and ran behind some bushes.

The driver got out, looked at the cattle in the back, then walked away to the front. When he came back a minute later, he was angry. "Damn it! To hell with everything!" he shouted, got back into the truck and drove off before Frank and Linda could do anything.

They stood in the dusty air and looked at each other.

"Where are we?" Frank said.

"I don't know. Somewhere in Kansas, I think. But look over there. There are some old buildings. It looks like an old Wild West town."

"Oh no!" Frank shouted suddenly.

"What? What's the matter?"

8	**dirt road**	nicht asphaltierte Straße
8	**dusty** ['dʌstɪ]	staubig
18	**hell**	Hölle
18	**to hell with ...**	zum Teufel mit ...
27	**what's the matter?**	was ist denn los?

"My hat is still on the truck."

"Oh, I thought it was something important," Linda said.

"It is, to me," Frank told her.

"Sorry, I didn't know," Linda said and smiled at Frank, and he smiled back at her.

"Well, let's see where we are," Linda said, and they walked over to the buildings.

"It's a ghost town," she said when they stood in a dirt street between two rows of old wooden houses. "I've heard of them."

"A ghost town? Ghosts?" Frank looked worried.

9 **row** [rəʊ] Reihe
9 **wooden** ['wʊdn] hölzern, aus Holz

And then they heard the voice. Someone was singing. It was a woman's voice.

"That's 'Don't fence me in'," Linda said.

"What?" Frank asked.

"The song she's singing. Come on, she's behind that building over there," Linda said.

When they had gone around the house, the friends found an older woman sitting on a porch. She was in her 50s and they soon learned that her name was Martha and that she was very surprised and glad to see them. "I don't get many visitors here," she said. "How did you get here?"

Linda told her about the truck.

"Oh, that's right. There's a waterhole over there. The cattle trucks sometimes use it, but it's dry now," she said and took them inside the old house. "This is where I live. I've been here for over six years now and I love it."

"Is there a telephone?" Frank asked her.

"No, I'm completely cut off from the outside world."

"You're all alone here then?" Linda asked, and Martha explained that she had been tired of living with other people. "So I came here to this ghost town – to Silver Heaven, Kansas. A long time ago there was a silver mine here, but when the silver was gone, all the people left – and now I'm the only one here."

They talked about everything then. When Linda said that she was running away, Martha didn't say anything. She just looked at her, but when she heard Frank's story, she looked puzzled.

8 **porch** [pɔ:tʃ] *(US)* eine Art Veranda
20 **to be tired of s.th.** etwas satt haben

"Why are they still after you?" she asked. "They could just go away and no one would catch them. Have you still got something of theirs, Frank?"

Now Frank looked puzzled. He thought about everything. "No," he said. "Nothing. They had my passport, but I have that back now."

After they had eaten, Frank said, "We must leave. I must find a telephone and the police. My parents and my aunt –"

"Hey, no police," Linda suddenly said. "They will take me back home."

"You *both* have to call your parents and let them know you are all right," Martha said. "But you can't do that from here. You have to get back –"

"Back to civilization," Frank said.

"Right," Martha laughed, and Linda smiled at him.

"We'll walk back to the road," she said.

"No, that's too far, and maybe those men are still there. I've got a better idea, but it won't work until tomorrow," Martha told them.

1 **to be after s.o.** hinter jdm her sein

Chapter 6

The next morning, Martha and the kids got up early. She put some home-made bread, dried meat and apples in a piece of cloth for them and tied it together.

"This is for you," she said. "I have lots of food here. Enough for months and months."

Then they left Silver Heaven together.

"We have to walk about a mile through the prairie," Martha explained. "Then we'll get to a railroad track There'll be a freight train at about 9 o'clock. It will slow down for a bend out there, and you'll be able to jump on. I hope you can do that."

"Of course," Frank said. "No problem."

"The next town will be Winslow. It's only a small place, but you can jump off there and go to the police. They'll help you. You, too, Linda."

Linda smiled at the woman but did not say anything.

With Smitty's help Pancho and Fats had found the cattle truck and stopped it.

"What do you want?" the driver asked. He was angry.

"We want to look in your truck," Pancho told him.

"What? Are you crazy?"

"We're looking for somebody," Fats tried to calm him.

3	**cloth** [klɒθ]	Tuch, Stoff
3	**to tie together**	zusammenbinden
8	**railroad** ['--] *(AE)*	Eisenbahn
8	**track**	*hier:* Eisenbahnschiene, -gleis
9	**freight** [freɪt] **train** *(AE)*	Güterzug
10	**bend**	Kurve

"Well, there isn't anybody here. You idiots can see that, can't you?" the driver shouted, but Pancho paid no attention to him and went to the back of the truck and looked in. "Just cattle," he called to the others.

"I told you," the driver said.

"Hey, wait. Look what I found." Pancho came back with Frank's hat.

"So he *was* here," Fats said.

"OK, tell us exactly where you've been," Pancho told the driver.

They heard the train long before they could see it. Its whistle filled the prairie. And when the train went into the bend and slowed down, Martha hugged them.

The train was very long. It just went on and on, and the children waited until they saw an open boxcar. Then they ran, faster and faster, and finally jumped and were on the train and waved back to Martha as it picked up speed again.

In the boxcar Frank and Linda sat on the floor and watched the prairie fly by through the open door.

"In Winslow you have to go to the police right away," Linda said. "They can help you."

"Come with me, Linda."

"I can't."

"Please."

"No! They will take me back home."

They were quiet then.

12	**whistle** ['wɪsl]	*hier:* Pfeifen, Pfiff
15	**boxcar** ['--] *(AE)*	Güterwagen
17	**to wave** [weɪv]	winken

"I've been thinking about something Martha said" Linda told him after a while. "Why are those men after you? You must have something they want."

"But I don't. The only thing I have is this pouch here," Frank said and took it from around his neck. "And I don't want that. I don't want anything from them." He took his passport and the ticket out, put them in his jeans pocket and threw the pouch out through the open door.

They were quiet again after that – until Frank said, "I want to go home. You should go home, too. Come to the police with me."

Linda shook her head and looked out of the door. "Was there anything in that pouch? I mean besides your passport and ticket?" she asked.

Now Frank shook his head. "No, just some paper at the bottom. That's all."

"What kind of paper?"

"I don't know. Just paper. Bags often have paper in them to keep their – er –"

"Their shape," Linda helped him with the word. "Yes, I know, but maybe there was something on the paper, something important."

Frank looked at her. "Maybe, but I don't think so. And it's gone now."

"Yes," Linda said and got up. She walked to the door and looked out – then pulled her head in again fast. "Hey, Frank, come here!"

Frank joined her at the door and looked out with her. The pouch was still there. It was hanging on a piece of metal and flapping in the wind.

20	**shape**	Form
30	**metal** ['metl]	
30	**to flap** [flæp]	*hier:* hin- und herwehen

"Quick, let's get it back," Linda said and leaned out. "Hold on to me."

"No, Linda, it's too dangerous," Frank told her, but she was already hanging out of the door, and Frank held onto her quickly.

The wind was strong as Linda stretched and tried to get the pouch – and just as it was about to fly off, she grabbed it, and Frank pulled her back in.

"Boy, that was close," she said.

"You'll see, it's only paper," Frank said to her — and then, as the train raced towards Winslow, they sat down again and opened the pouch.

Pancho, Fats and Smitty, too, were waiting for the train in Winslow.

"I'm sure he's on that train," Pancho said.

"He has to be!" Smitty said, "or you two are going to be in real trouble."

"He has to be," Fats said. "That woman didn't tell us anything, but we found tracks, so she took him to the train."

"What if he doesn't get off here?" Pancho asked.

"Then we'll get on the train and find him," Smitty said.

For a long moment the friends just sat there and looked at the stones on the floor.

"Well," Linda finally said, "everything's clear now. I'm sure they're diamonds, and they want them back."

6	**to stretch** [stretʃ]	sich strecken
7	**to be about to do s.th.**	im Begriff sein etwas zu tun
9	**close** [kləʊs]	*hier:* knapp
19	**track** [træk]	*hier:* Spur

"What do you think, Linda? How much are they?"

"You mean, how much are they *worth*?"

"Yes, worth."

Linda played with all the shiny stones in front of them, then said, "I don't know, but you have to take them to the police now. Those men will not stop hunting you as long as you have them. And you will be OK here. They don't know you're on the train."

"Yes, I will go, in Winslow," Frank said and looked at her.

"No," Linda said. "I won't come with you."

Frank was unhappy. He liked Linda – a lot. She was like a sister his own age – and she had problems. He wished he could help her, but now they would never see each other again.

2 **worth** [wɜ:θ] wert

Chapter 7

When the train stopped in Winslow, Frank looked out and when he didn't see anyone, he got off quickly. Linda came to the door, waved to him and then went back into the boxcar.

Frank looked around. There wasn't even a station here – just a place for the train to stop and a little town on the other side of the tracks. Frank crossed them and walked towards the houses.

Behind a wooden building near him, Pancho, Fats and Smitty were waiting.

"Let's get him now," Pancho said and started to run out.

"No, you idiot," Smitty said and held him back. "Somebody might see us."

"Yeah, but we have to get him before he can go to the police."

"Just wait."

Frank was on Main Street now. It looked just like the ones he had seen in films: it was very wide, cars were parked on both sides and there were shops in low buildings on both sides, too. Some cars were going through town very slowly and there were a few people on the sidewalks. He liked the town. It looked so peaceful.

7 **to cross** [krɒs] überqueren
18 **wide** [waɪd] breit
19 **low** [ləʊ] niedrig
22 **peaceful** ['pi:sfʊl] friedlich

A young woman with a little girl came by then, and Frank spoke to her. "Can you tell me the way to the police station, please?" he asked her. It was a sentence from his English book, but now he didn't even have to think about it.

The woman smiled. "Sure, honey. It's –"

"Mama, I know that boy," her little girl said then. "I saw his picture on TV."

"Sure you did, Peggy," her mother laughed. "She watches too much TV," she said to Frank. "Now, young man, you go down this street and then –"

"But, Mama, I really did –"

"Now you hush, Peggy, when I'm talking to somebody! OK, young man, down this street and then you turn north at the second traffic light. It'll be the low red building on the west side. Have you got that?"

Frank said 'yes' and thanked her and left fast before Peggy could start again.

"We have to move now," Pancho said. "I'm sure he asked her about the police station. That's where he's going. It's down that way. I saw it when we drove in."

"OK, OK, just wait till he's off the main street. Let's get to the car."

"It'll be too late. The police station's just around the corner."

"Let's hurry then," Smitty barked at the others.

1	**to come by**	vorbeikommen
5	**honey** ['hʌnɪ]	*hier:* Schatz, Schätzchen
12	**to hush** [hʌʃ]	still sein
18	**to move**	*hier:* handeln

Frank walked down the street fast. Now what had she said? The second traffic light – and turn north. Which way was that? Frank tried to remember what he had learned about the sun. There was a big clock on the building in front of him. It was almost noon. Frank looked up at the big blue sky. The sun should be right in the south now. Yes, there it was to his left. So north was to the right. He walked on, got to the second traffic light and went around the corner.

It all happened very fast after that: Frank came around the corner, a car door opened suddenly, someone pulled him in and put a hand over his mouth, the door closed and the car raced away.

At the police station about 100 feet down the street two police cars were parked and everything was quiet.

"Hey, that was close," Frank heard Fats say next to him, and on his other side Smitty said, "OK, where are the diamonds?"

"Thought we were gone, didn't you?" Pancho laughed.

"Shut up and drive," Smitty shouted. "Let him talk."

"Look what I've got here, Frank," Fats said and gave him his baseball hat. "We found it."

Frank took it and put it on. "Thanks," he said to Fats.

"Hey, what is this?" Smitty was angry. "A family reunion? OK now, boy, where are the diamonds?"

"I don't know what you mean," Frank said.

"Hey, you've learned some more English," Fats said and smiled at him. "Great."

5 **noon** [nu:n] Mittag
24 **family reunion** [ri:ˈju:njən] Familientreffen

"Never mind that! Now where's the pouch?" Smitty shouted and grabbed Frank.

"The what?" Frank tried to look puzzled.

"The little bag you took, you idiot!"

"Oh that. I threw it away."

"You what!?" Pancho turned around, and the car nearly went off the road.

"Hey, watch the road!" Fats told him.

"Threw it away?" Smitty said in a funny way. "Well, you had it when you were in that ghost town. We know that. And your passport was in it. You didn't throw that away?"

"No, I've got that right here," Frank started to take it out of his pocket, but Smitty grabbed his hand and took it out for him. "But I threw the pouch out of the train," Frank added.

"Sure you did, but you took your passport out first," the thin man held it up, "and that means you've got the rest, too. Stop the car somewhere, Pancho. We're going to search him," Smitty ordered.

When Pancho had found a good place to stop, the men searched Frank. He fought them, but they held him down and in the end Fats found the diamonds in his back pocket.

"All right, then," Smitty smiled for the first time. "We've got them. We're back in business. Let's get to the plane, Pancho. Fast."

"Right, boss. We'll leave this rented car in the bushes somewhere and then we'll be off to Mexico."

19 **to search** [sɜːtʃ] durchsuchen
19 **to order** ['--] *hier:* befehlen
25 **in business** ['bɪznɪs] im Geschäft

"Shut up, you idiot! Don't tell him where we're going," Fats said.

"Doesn't matter," Smitty answered. "This time we'll do the job right. He won't be able to talk to anybody."

Pancho raced down the road another mile, then turned off onto a dirt road with small trees on both sides. He drove a bit further until they came to an open place. The plane was there.

"Just leave the car over there and let's go. Everything is going to be all right now," Smitty was very happy.

"Yeah," Pancho laughed and showed all his big teeth. "For us, but not for him," he said as they pulled Frank over to the plane.

Inside the plane, Smitty went to the cockpit right away while his partners took Frank to the back. Smitty tried to start the plane, but the engine wouldn't turn over. He tried again. "Damn!" he said. "There's a problem!"

"There's a problem back here, too," a strange voice said behind him.

Smitty turned around fast – and saw a policeman with a gun.

Outside the plane, the police handcuffed Smitty and his men, and took them over to some police cars, which were now there.

16 **to turn over**	*hier:* starten
18 **strange**	*hier:* unbekannt
20 **to turn around**	sich umdrehen
21 **gun** [gʌn]	*hier:* Pistole
22 **to handcuff** ['hændkʌf]	Handschellen anlegen

"Great," an older police officer said to Frank. "We found you, and you're OK! And we got these guys with all their diamonds and furs. You know there's a big reward for this."

"Reward?" Frank asked.

"Money for catching them," somebody said behind him. Frank turned around. It was Linda, and she was smiling at him.

"Linda!" Frank shouted, and they hugged each other.

"This young lady is the one who saved you," the police officer said. "Maybe you two should talk."

3 **reward** [rɪ'wɔːd] Belohnung

"It's good to see you, Frank," she laughed.

"But you were on that train."

"Yes, but as it was leaving, I saw those three guys. So I jumped out and went to the police as fast as I could."

"She sure did," the police officer said. "She's one smart girl."

"But now, Linda, the police will take you –" Frank started but didn't go on.

5 **smart** [smɑːt] *hier:* intelligent

Chapter 8

At Aunt Trudy's house in Oklahoma City Frank and his parents were together again. His mother couldn't stop hugging and kissing him and everybody was talking in German.

But then, after everybody had calmed down a bit, Aunt Trudy spoke to Frank in English, "You know, the police have told us a lot, but now I want to hear everything from you."

"Right," Frank said, and when he started telling them everything in English, his parents just sat there with big eyes.

"I don't see what the problem is," Aunt Trudy said later. "His English is just fine."

In the afternoon, there was a phone call.

"It's for you, Frank," his aunt said. They only spoke English to each other.

Frank went to the phone. Who could it be? He didn't know anyone here.

"Hello," he said and then he heard a voice he knew. It was Linda – and she was at home again.

They talked for a long time then, and then Linda's mother wanted to talk to his mother. "My mom's English isn't very good," Frank told her, and in the end Aunt Trudy went to the phone.

"They're going to fly here to Oklahoma because they want to meet you and thank you," she said afterwards.

"Thank us?" Frank asked.

"Thank *you*, because Linda is at home again."

3 **to kiss** küssen

Linda and her parents arrived at Will Roger's Airport in Oklahoma City the next day. They stayed in Oklahoma for four days and a lot of things were arranged.

For one thing, it was decided that the two families would share the reward.

"What's a reward?" Frank's father had asked in English, and Frank explained it to him.

"A reward?" his mother said, and when she found out how much it was, she said a lot more – in German.

"I guess that will pay for everything," Aunt Trudy smiled.

They also talked about Linda and her school problem and found a solution ...

Everything was great and everyone had a good time. And after Linda and her family had left, Frank and his parents spent the rest of the Easter holidays in Oklahoma with Aunt Trudy and enjoyed themselves. It was a real holiday.

In the first English lesson after the holidays Frau Peters stood in front of her class and smiled. "Well, everybody, what did you do in the holidays? I hope you didn't just watch TV and that you learned some English, too. Who is going to tell us about their holiday first?"

Nobody raised a hand, but Frank sat there with a baseball hat in his hands and smiled at her.

He probably didn't even understand my question, Frau Peters thought, but then Frank's hand went up.

Everybody looked at him. That had never happened before in English.

3	**to arrange** [ə'reɪndʒ]	
5	**to share** [ʃeə]	sich etwas teilen
12	**solution** [sə'lu:ʃn]	Lösung
22	**to raise** [reɪz]	(hoch)heben

"Yes?" Frau Peters said.

"Perhaps I can tell you and the class about some of the things that happened to me," Frank said.

Frau Peters' mouth fell open, and the class became very quiet.

And then he started telling them.

"Wow!" Michael said and then went on in German.

Frau Peters told him to say it again in English, but he couldn't.

"They could make a film about that," Jessica said.

Frank looked at her. "Well, some American TV people talked to us about that. But I don't know. Maybe."

Everybody talked then, in German, until Frau Peters told them to stop.

"But the best part is that Linda is going to be in our class next year," Frank said.

"What do you mean?" one of the girls asked.

"Linda is going to stay with me next year. She's going to be my exchange partner for the whole year. She helped me with my English ..."

"She certainly did," Frau Peters said and sat down. There were tears in her eyes again.

"... and I'm going to help her to learn German. We all can," Frank said, and everybody got really excited then and started talking and asking Frank all kinds of questions ...

A class project

Here is a project the whole class can do:
a magazine presentation of the story – in English.

Here's what you will need:

- a map
- a main article
- interviews
- smaller articles
- *fact files
- an *editorial/leader
- good *headlines
- photos

Who should do what?

1. *The map*

- One of you should make a map that shows where the story takes place.
- You could copy or scan the map from this reader or from another book, from a CD-Rom or the Internet ... or you can draw your own map.
- Put in the names of the states and towns and draw in the different sections of the trip west, perhaps in different colors. You could even draw a little car, a plane, a truck and a train ...
- You could do all this very professionally with a computer.
- You will need a short text under the map and perhaps a sentence or two to explain things.

fact file	Info-Box
editorial/leader	Leitartikel
headline	Überschrift

2. *The main article*

- Someone must write the main story. This will be like a long summary. The article should be about all the important things; it should not give too many details.
- Perhaps more than one person can do this. Someone can write about Germany and New York City, someone else about going west, etc.
- You can refer to the map in these as well as in the other articles.

3. *Interviews*

- You could interview some of the characters in the story.
- Here is a list of the ones you might want to use:
  - the parents (especially after the adventure; translate into English)
  - the police (What can they say about the *crooks and about Frank and Linda?)
  - the crooks (Are they all the same? What about Fats?)
  - the Korean (What can he say about America?)
  - Frank and Linda (What do they think about all this? What about their plans?)
  - Frau Peters (What does she think about Frank now? And what about the fact that Linda will come to Germany?)

Can you think of anyone else you could interview?

crook Verbrecher

4. *Smaller articles*

- Instead of writing interviews you could put some of this information into shorter articles.
- You would then concentrate on one person or one special problem.
- For these articles as well as for the interviews above you will have to *invent some things, for example how old the crooks are, their last names, where they are from, their family background, their police record, etc.

5. *Fact files*

- Magazines often use fact files (in boxes) beside articles to give more information about special aspects of the story.
- Here are some aspects of the story that you could write about in a fact file:
  - crime in America
  - immigration (the Korean, Pancho; legal, illegal)
  - diamonds
  - ghost towns in the US (perhaps with a photo from the Internet)
  - young people who run away from home (problems with parents, school, etc.)
- Where can you find this information?
  - in an encyclopedia or other *reference book
  - on the Internet
  - Perhaps your teacher can give you some material.
- Can you think of any other aspect of the story that could be explained in a fact file?

to invent erfinden
reference book Nachschlagewerk

6. *An editorial/leader*

- Someone could write an editorial. The other articles should be objective, but in an editorial you can give your opinion.
- What could you have an opinion about?
  - What should be done with the criminals?
  - Was it right to send Frank to the US on his own?
  - Can you think of anything else?

7. *Good headlines*

- Can someone in the class write really clever headlines?
- They should be short and interesting *in order to get the reader's attention right away.
- And what about *subheadings? You may want to use them to guide the reader through an article.

8. *Photos*

- Someone could take pictures of people and use the photos in the magazine.
- Who could be Frank? Who Linda? And the crooks? A police officer?
- A computer and scanner would be useful for this.

9. *The layout*

- One or two of you should work on the layout.
- You can look at magazines to get ideas on how to arrange pieces on a page.

in order to um ... zu ...
subheading Zwischentitel

- What *fonts/typeface should you use? (Perhaps one for the headlines and a different one for the texts, with perhaps a special one for the fact files. But be careful, don't use too many or the magazine will look like a comic.)
- If you want to have pages opposite each other, make sure they look good together.
- This would be a good job for someone who can work with a computer (and a scanner).

10. *The boss*
- Someone needs to be the editor.
- She or he must make sure that all the pieces are finished on time, that they fit together and don't overlap.
- The editor makes suggestions and corrections.
- The editor may also be the one who writes the editorial.

11. *Printing*
- If you want to print all this as a *booklet, someone will have to be *in charge.
- If you can't do everything with a computer, you may want to use a photocopier to change the size of some pieces.
- If you want to have text on both sides of the paper, you will have to plan this.

Perhaps you have some more ideas ...?

Have fun!

font/typeface Schriftart
booklet Broschüre
in charge verantwortlich